The Not Philosophies

An Introduction to the Philosophies of Not and Authorism

Written by

Thomas Vaughn

The Not Philosophies

An Introduction to the Philosophies of Not and Authorism

By
Thomas Vaughn

ISBN: 978-1-7372750-1-5

Cover art and book design
by Thomas Vaughn

TNP_2023_0206_0935

This text provides a brief description of what is wrong with some of the existing systems of belief (primarily in the forms of religions) and a brief explanation of the Not Philosophies (which are collectively, the Philosophy of Not and the ideology of Authorism). The Not Philosophies may be used as a secular approach to moral living with deeper meaning and purpose but without the requirement of god(s) or religion(s).

Contents

PURPOSE

This document originally started as a manifesto of sorts. It was a way for me to publish (in brief) what I believe is wrong with the existing systems of belief (primarily in the form of religions), and at the same time introduce some ideas that might be used instead.

Because we live in a globalized, interdependent, technological society which offers us a myriad of competing philosophies and systems of belief that vie for our adherence, it can be difficult to know where to start. Not is the most fundamental base to reality and as such, one can use the Not Philosophies, which are grounded in logic, reason, and intuition to build (or add to) one's unshakeable foundation and structure of belief.

Beyond this fundamental base, The Not Philosophies outline my thoughts on where gods and religions fit in with reality while offering a way to *be* in the world without having to bow down to someone (or something) who knows just as little or less than you do about the universe and beyond.

These philosophies are offered as splinters of truth that you might use to add to your own "bundle of truth" as you continue to blaze your way through time and space on your inner and outer journeys through life.

◆ ◆ ◆

AUTHORITY

Who has authority over you?

Your parents? Your partner or spouse? Your mullah, rabbi, priest, or preacher? Your manager, supervisor, or boss? Everyone? No one? The police? The government? The gods?

When I ask "who has authority over you," I do not mean in the shallows of the day-to-day drudgery of everyday life. I am not talking about who creates your report card, signs your paycheck or approves your project.

I am talking about something much deeper than that. Or much higher than that, depending on your viewpoint.

I am talking about your true self. Your deep, inner-self. The self that matters most. I am talking about that part of you that is aware of the fact that you are aware. The you that is the *awareness of its own awareness* – the voice in your mind that is reading this to you. Or perhaps the one who is listening to this being read. Your spirit-consciousness.

Who can tell you what you should do with yourself at any given time during the day? Who can tell you how to act? Who can tell you what to say or what to think?

When I talk about authorization, I am talking about validation; a sanction for being who you are.

How do you know that you have a right to be here?

It is my assertion that there is only one authority who can authorize your being. That being is you. And it's only you.

There are many reasons we seek authorization from outside of ourselves, not the least of which is that humanity has been seeking external authorization for millennia and it has become our modus operandi.

Our parents learned it from their parents; their parents learned it from their parents; etc., ad infinitum. It goes back in time beyond recorded civilization.

Like most everyone else, I grew up having learned from my parents that only something outside of myself could validate me. In my case, as a Christian child, it was only God who could sanction my existence. I was taught that we were created by God and therefore God owned us and we owed our entire lives to God.

If I were created by some higher power, and for some reason, shouldn't I fulfill my destiny and accomplish that directive which I had been created to accomplish?

If I am not actively working toward accomplishing that which I was created to accomplish, am I still okay? Or am I failing in some way?

Or, as some of the major religions of modern times posit, was I created broken and damaged to begin with and therefore need to spend my life desperately seeking some kind of redemption for having been created as a damaged person filled with sin?

I must admit, from as early as I can remember, I could not understand why my parents, other adults, and church leaders, did not devote their lives to God. After all, the way they talked, shouldn't we all just spend every waking moment praising God and being grateful for everything "He" had given us?

The other thing that mystified me was our purpose. No matter how many people I asked, and how many ways they tried to explain it, nobody was ever able to explain to me why God created us to begin with. It made absolutely no sense to me that God would create me broken and filled with sin and then punish me for being that which it had created. Nor could I fathom a being capable of creating all life and the entire cosmos-and-beyond for the only purpose of having humans tell him how amazing he was.

And if we were not created solely to "praise God," as for why humanity *was* created, none of the answers I have heard from any religion make sense to me. I have heard some pretty good explanations from science fiction which make a lot more sense, but certainly nothing from "The Bible."

As a result of my curiosity and unanswered (or unsatisfactorily answered) questions, I was never able to feel fully *authorized* by my God. I tried. God knows, I tried (sorry, I had to). But despite praying fervently, sincerely, and frequently, I did not feel like I was "ok." I did not feel like I belonged here. In fact, for many years, I felt I was an imposter on this planet, that I was somehow displaced among the humans and maybe I was not even one of them.

I wanted to believe in their god(s). In fact, that desire to believe is still with me and is part of the Religion Guilt Complex that so many of us recovering religious people have to fight through. One of the reasons I wanted so passionately to believe was that *if it were true*, everything would be so much easier.

If it were true, it would mean that there is a being who knows me all the way to my core but loves me anyway. It would mean that I have a definitive purpose to my life. It would mean that all of this pain, suffering and horror in the world has a meaning. It would state definitively that order wins out over chaos.

As I progressed through my teen years, it became apparent that my Mormon upbringing could not answer my questions. And that's saying a lot because the Mormons are expert at coming up with some fairly intellectually satisfying responses to some of the bigger questions. But, like all of the organized religions, they root themselves in scriptures, and if you've ever read any of the scriptures then you know there are so many unanswered questions! And it seems for every answered question, two or three more questions pop up requiring new answers.

Seeking elsewhere, I started with some of the other sects of Christianity. No help there. I then looked into Judaism, Buddhism, Hinduism, Zoroastrianism, Islam, and even entertained science fiction ideas such as Scientology and other stories that tried to explain what is going on all around us.

Then there was Atheism. Atheism seemed to be the obvious alternative to all of that religion-seeking, but Atheism did not have the answers either.

What I did not realize throughout all of that searching was that I was actually seeking something deeper than the answers to The Mysteries. If you had asked me, "What are you searching for?" on any given year throughout the thirty or so years I was seeking, I would have told you, "I am searching for the answers to The Mysteries. The most significant of those mysteries being,

Where did we come from?

Why are we here?
What is the meaning of life?
Is there purpose, and if so, what is that purpose?"

But what I finally came to realize when I wrote the first book of Not, in early 2020, was that during all those years I was seeking answers to The Mysteries, there was something even deeper and more fundamental that I was seeking without even knowing I was seeking it.

I was seeking authorization.

And more specifically, I was seeking *external* authorization.

I was seeking external authorization for my own being. I was no different from any other human. I was brought up to believe that authorization for being came from outside of myself – it is an unspoken undercurrent whispered (but without sound) constantly to our souls, that tells us that only something outside of ourselves can make us whole.

It is not our fault. It is not our parents' fault. It is not the fault of organized religion either. There is no fault in it because it just is. It is, perhaps, a right of passage on the path toward spiritual liberation. It's a byproduct of the way we *are* in this world.

As babies, we are raw instinct. We desire something and we scream until we get it. And it is as babies that we begin to learn that everything we need comes from outside of ourselves. The desire or need for something comes from within and the appeasement of that desire or need comes from outside.

Initially this applies to every single need we have. As we grow into toddlers, then children, then teenagers, etc., we begin to learn how to appease these inner needs and desires ourselves. In fact, it might be argued that the primary duty of the parent is to teach the child exactly that skill: how to fend for itself – how to find solutions for her problems on her own. So that when the child is ready to leave the nest, she can interoperate in society, not just holding her own, but excelling and achieving even greater things than her parents had achieved.

It is quite natural that we would learn to presume that authorization for being could be found outside of ourselves. After all, that's where everything else came from. Sustenance, information, hugs, and kisses – all came from outside. Many people find this external authorization in the form of another person or an organization and hold on to it (perhaps too tightly).

Some get it from their parents, and as long as the parents still provide it, they are content. Some get it from their spouse, or partner. Again, this might seem to be effective as long as the outside source continues to provide it. The list of where it can come from is what I started this "Authority" section with and there are countless people who seem content in obtaining their authorization from one of those external sources.

The problem with those external sources is that they are not real *sources,* and deep down inside, we know that. So when the question bubbles up from the mind, or the soul, "Am I okay?" and we locate an external source that tells us, "Yes, you are okay," we know that there is still something amiss. There, deep within, is a hint of doubt.

When we get our external authorization from people, it always comes with a modicum of doubt. Is this person saying I am ok because they have an ulterior motive? Probably. After all, other people only know the aspects of you which you have tried to share with them. Nobody can really know you fully. They can never know you as well as you know yourself.

What about god(s) then? Authorization from god(s) is wonderful as long as you have an absolute fixed faith in the god and have absolutely no doubts as to that god's existence and her love for you. If there is doubt, then the authorization you get from that god is also in doubt. And this lingering doubt causes a subtle anxiety that ripples throughout your being.

There is only one pure source of authorization for being – only one place you can find it. It is from within yourself. The fact that the ultimate authorization for being can only come from within is a secret known to some of the Gnostic and Mystic spiritual practices dating back hundreds and even thousands of years.

But there is a deeper secret that is known to very few. The deeper secret is that you do not need to be authorized at all.

Deep within your mind or spirit – or *spirit-consciousness* – is your true self. This is the non-intellectual self – the awareness of your own awareness. This self does not need authorization because it is like a star shining in the black of space. It burns brightly, emanating you-energy into the multiverse without asking if it is allowed to or apologizing for having done so. It does not need permission to exist. It has a right to be here simply because it *is* here. It is an axiom. It is you. And no different than the sun and the moon, you have a right to be here.

When we can tap into that deepest, purest core of ourselves, we can experience the bliss of being. I think this is what it might feel like to be a sun. We just have much shorter lifespans (and more self-doubt) than they do.

But until you fully understand that you no longer need authorization for being, there may be times when you find yourself seeking it. In times such as these, you can find authorization by "dropping down" into your deepest self and becoming one with the fire which burns within. This is the same fire that many spiritual practices refer to as the "divine fire," or the "divine spark," or the "divinity within."

This leads me to the curse of organized religion. This beast called, Organized Religion, claims *it* can provide us with the authorization for being that we can only truly find on our own, deep within our own being. Organized Religion not only makes this claim but promises it! Either in this life or the next.

◆ ◆ ◆

ORGANIZED RELIGION

There are two deceptions that all organized religions perpetrate no matter where the religion is in the world, how old the religion is or how many people are card-carrying members: absolute knowledge and absolute authority.

ABSOLUTE KNOWLEDGE

All religions claim to have not just a greater understanding of, but rather an *absolute* knowledge of, "that which is hidden." I put that in quotes because "that which is hidden" is a good way to define the word "occult." One could say that, "religion claims to have absolute knowledge of that which is occulted." There's a contradiction here that I will circle back to in a moment.

But however you want to refer to it, what I'm talking about by that "which is hidden" or "the occult" is everything to do with "the beyond." This means life after death, life before life, ghosts, gods, demons, angels, divination, resurrection, eternal bliss or damnation, heaven, hell, purgatory, the simulation, the supernatural, the origin of the universe, the meaning of life, magic, extra (or inter or intra)-dimensional life and/or being, etc., and so forth.

Anything that cannot yet be explained but teases or intrigues us with the questions of what, when, why, how, or where. What is going on here? When will we find out? Why are we here? How did it all come to be this way? Where is it all going? We can refer to these kinds of questions collectively as "The Mysteries."

Any religion worth its salt will claim to have definitive answers to these questions. A doctrine that details the answers to The Mysteries will be part of their scriptures. Or if they do not have doctrine that details the answers, then another angle might be that their holy people (priests, etc.) can *deduce* the answers to The Mysteries *from* their scriptures. To derive the answers, they might employ divine intervention or tap into deep esoteric knowledge of their scriptures from years of prayer, study, and/or meditation.

In any event, each religion claims to have absolute knowledge that trumps all of the others.

We should address the contradiction I mentioned above before moving on. The term, occult, or "that which is hidden," implies that someone, somewhere, knows the things which are hidden from the rest of us. After all, someone had to do the hiding in order for the knowledge to be hidden to begin with. Who knows these things? Each religion will tell you that the ones who know the things that you don't know – the things that are hidden from your view – are the priests, preachers, or holy people of the religion in question. And implicit in that absolute knowledge is the promise that some of these supernatural and deep secrets of the universe may be shared with you if you join the club and adhere to the rules, learn the rituals, participate in the ceremonies, recite the prayers, do as you are told, and above all, pay your tithing. Yes, give them money.

There is no such thing as absolute knowledge. Neither science, nor religion (or any combination thereof) has absolute knowledge. This is quite evident in observing how the older religions of the world continually change in an attempt to stay relevant (and legal) as the world changes around them. For instance, once it became illegal to burn people alive for practicing science, the Catholic church altered their interpretation of their bible so they would not have to break the law by torturing to death those people who asked too many questions. That which is absolute, cannot change. And contrariwise, if something can change, it can't be absolute.

ABSOLUTE AUTHORITY

Even more astonishing than the claim of absolute knowledge, is the claim of absolute authority. One of the most fundamental basics of all organized religion is the astounding claim that they have authority over you or that they know who does.

The argument is airtight and extremely simple. Basically, it goes something like this: Some supernatural creative force (usually called "God(s)" created everything, including you. Because you were created by this godhead, you owe your life to the godhead. The godhead holds authority over you and since you cannot communicate directly with the god(s), but the holy people of the religion *can*, you need to acknowledge that the holy people have authority over you as a proxy for your (their) god(s).

How is it that the holy people have this authority? Well, the god(s) gave it to them, of course. (And you cannot argue with the creator(s) of the universe.) And how do we know that the god(s) vested the holy people with such authority? Well, the holy people tell us so.

They have an airtight case. Don't worry about the fact that it is a case of circular reasoning and therefore completely invalid, illogical, and irrational. If you feel concerned by this you are probably asking too many questions, thinking too much (my personal favorite) or not exhibiting enough faith. In other words, believe it because you're told to believe it.

The solution to your (probably) heretical doubt is for you to double down on your payments (in actual cash), pray for forgiveness and strengthen your faith.

THE ANGRY ATHEIST

It is usually at this point in the discussion that the author of a text like this one begins to start sounding angry and a rant about the dangers of faith, blind faith, the corruption of the priesthood (pick any religion for this one) etc. ensues. I am not going to do this. (But then again, I am not an atheist, either.)

Anger is a perfectly valid stage of grief and should not be ignored but anger is not necessarily helpful in furthering one's understanding, nor is it helpful in finding the spiritual path to self.

Atheism, as a way of looking at the world, is not the only alternative when one acknowledges that there is no such thing as absolute knowledge, and that no external entity can authorize your being.

This might be a good time for me to come clean and just say outright: 1. I am not an atheist, and 2. all religions are false. However, on that second point, religions *can* be true to those who believe in them. But what is true for you is not necessarily true for me. This includes Atheism, for those who identify with this label.

The "angry atheist" is often angry because she feels she was tricked into believing something that she later comes to believe is no longer true (or worse, was never true). She feels like she has been deceived or made the fool. If she grew up in a religion where her parents and peers were staunch believers it can be even worse, because she probably rooted her entire structure and foundation of belief in the dogma of the religion she was raised in.

The time comes when she realizes that it was all based on a lie. That none of it was real. Her structure of belief collapses and her foundation of belief shatters.

This can bring on far worse feelings than just anger or rage over having been "deceived." When your foundation of belief is shattered, the whole world shatters with it. In a case like this, one must construct an entirely new foundation and structure of belief. One must first start from the ground up, slowly rebuilding their foundation of belief until it is solid enough to support a structure. Once that work is done, they must then start in on rebuilding their structure of belief. This can be a vulnerable, lengthy, scary, and painful process.

I have come a long way in my journey and coming to terms with my own anger (sometimes rage) from various events from my childhood is one of the things I've had to work through. Wait. Honestly, it is one of the things I continue to work through even today. I have made tremendous strides, become very successful in society, and I am generally "happy," but even with all the progress I have made, I still have the occasional flash of anger – and for the briefest of moments, sometimes even a flicker of rage.

There are times, in my day-to-day life, that I will pass a sign or a building that advertises some religion's absolute knowledge and authority and the unspoken expectation that I should bow down to this absolute authority and allow myself to be guided by them and their god(s). Or worse, that I am making a mistake by not bowing down to them and their god(s), or worse yet, that I am somehow harming myself or others by not doing what they say. The thing that sparks my anger is the presumption of absolute knowledge. How can they make such a bold assertion that they and they alone are the *only* rightful keepers of the secret truth of the universe?

In fact, it was one of those brief flashes of anger that inspired me to write this text. As a response to my own anger at someone making such a definitive claim of absolute authority, I felt compelled to write this. Not just compelled, but even that not writing this would be irresponsible or negligent.

It is my hope that by drawing your attention to the Philosophy of Not, I can provide you with an anchor or a cornerstone in your own foundation of belief that nobody can damage or take away from you. This knowledge is not hidden or occulted. You don't have to "join" to take it. It's right there in the plain sight of science, reason, and intuition.

◆ ◆ ◆

WHAT IS NOT?

So, what is Not, anyway?

I have borrowed the word, "not," from the English language and made it a proper noun. In borrowing this word, I have not changed the meaning you already know. It is exactly what it sounds like. It is what most of us think of as "nothing." But in turning it into the proper noun, "Not," I have added some more to this nothingness (or taken more away) that I need to explain.

In order to describe Not, I would like to start with one of the four attributes of Not: coldness.

COLDNESS

Coldness does not exist.

You might respond, "Of course it exists!"

Yes, you're right. It can be cold outside, in the refrigerator or in deep space. Allow me to explain what I mean.

What I mean by saying that coldness does not exist, is that by itself, coldness does not exist as thing which can be manipulated, carried, or added to or removed from a system.

We cannot take a bit of coldness and add it to a system to make that system colder.

For me, the first counter argument that comes to mind is ice. Isn't ice a bit of coldness that we add to a system (a drink) to make the system colder?

Practically speaking, that's certainly true. But *actually*, what is happening is that the ice is not *adding* cold to the liquid, but rather it is drawing heat *out* of the liquid (and into itself). And as a result of taking on this heat, the ice begins to melt and the liquid around the ice becomes colder.

I'm talking about thermodynamics and heat transfer. The way heat transfer works is that warmth will always move to that which is colder than itself. This is why air that is warm moves to the areas of the air which are colder – thus the reason we have breezes and wind.

You might ask, "So what? What difference does it make if it's the warmth moving to the cold or the cold moving to the warmth?"

In our everyday lives, it usually doesn't matter. But the difference is real, and it is significant.

The significance of this is that the *warmth* is what we can control. The *warmth* is what we can contain, carry, add, and remove from the system.

If we add warmth to a system, the system becomes warmer. If we remove warmth from a system, the system becomes colder. Either way, it is warmth that we are adding and removing, not coldness.

There are two more common counter arguments I would like to address: a refrigerator and space.

In the case of a refrigerator, you might argue that it is cold inside the refrigerator and that when you place food inside, the refrigerator moves coldness into the food. But this is not the case. True to the laws of thermodynamics, the refrigerator is not producing cold and adding it to the food. Instead, the refrigerator is removing warmth from inside. Thus, when you place some food in the refrigerator, the refrigerator begins to remove the warmth from the food and that warmth is sent outside the refrigerator. Put your hand near the back and you will feel the warmth pouring out. (The same is true if you place your hand over an air conditioner condenser fan outside a building on a hot summer day. You will feel the warmth that the air conditioner is removing from the building). You see? Warmth is what the refrigerator is manipulating in order to arrive at a certain level of coldness.

What about space? Isn't the temperature of space called "absolute zero?" This is the coldest temperature there is, right? I used to think that. But space has a couple of surprises. Absolute zero *is* the coldest temperature but space is ever so slightly warmer than that. Apparently, space, even in the most "empty" and remote parts of it, has some quantum activity. Stranger, perhaps, and easy to forget even after you've learned it once or twice, is that space is not a 'lack of stuff' but rather an actual substance. Space is made of something. Space is some kind of material that is actually expanding. What it is made of is still up for debate. Part of it, though, among other things, is evidently dark matter and/or dark energy. So, yes, space is about as cold as it gets, but no, space is not perfect coldness devoid of all warmth.

Remember I started this discussion on coldness by claiming that coldness, as a thing that might exist independently of other things, does not exist. Over the last few paragraphs, I have argued that coldness does not exist. But I have also argued that if we could remove all warmth, we would have nothing left *but* coldness. Thus, my argument is really twofold: One, that coldness does not exist, and two, that coldness must exist. Paradox is prevalent in truth. As something which cannot exist and therefore must exist, coldness is one of the four core precepts of Not.

Coldness does not exist, but because warmth exists, coldness must exist. One might make the argument that this is simply the nature of naming things. For instance, in order for there to be a front, there must be a back or in order for there to be an outside, there must also be an inside. In other words, that warmth versus coldness is merely a matter of semantics. But that is not the case. You can achieve varying levels of coldness by altering the warmth, but no amount of altering the "front" of something will make the "back" be less "back" than it already is. Front and back are very black and white definitions. Conceptually, coldness and warmth are not dualities like front and back or inside and outside.

Having these two attributes (1. a mandate to exist and 2. being a core precept of Not), coldness is a base attribute of existence that is "always there." And on top of this base precept, warmth can be added or subtracted. But underneath the warmth will always be this perfect and pure coldness that cannot be moved, altered, or affected in any way. Absolute coldness is pure, perfect, and exists independently of warmth.

Underneath all warmth, will always be this base precept, "coldness." And the only way to experience it would be to remove all the warmth. Removing all warmth, however, is not possible. As such, we can never achieve perfect coldness. We can never arrive at this core, pure and perfect base precept.

But let's, just for the sake of argument, say that such a perfect and pure coldness *could* exist. If it really could exist, we could never know about it.

This is because of the Observer Effect. The fact that just by virtue of observation, the observer alters the thing which is being observed. Measuring the air pressure in a tire is a good example of this. Let's say you have a tire with a pressure of 33.6 PSI. When you press the tire gauge onto the valve, there is a slight hiss as some air leaks out. Now the pressure is 33.5 PSI (and that's the number that now shoes up on the gauge). Removing the gauge might produce another slight hiss and now that you have finished measuring the tire, the tire pressure is 33.4 PSI, even though the gauge-reading is still at 33.5 PSI. You see, just by observing the tire pressure (which was 33.6) you have altered the original tire pressure from 33.6 PSI to 33.4 PSI. You caused the tire pressure to change twice and ironically your tire gauge reading of 33.5 PSI does not capture either one of the changes you caused by measuring the pressure to begin with, nor does it reflect the actual tire pressure once you finished taking your measurement. By "observing" the pressure, you have changed it.

The same is true with coldness. By attempting to measure perfect coldness, your measuring device would necessarily introduce some warmth, thereby "ruining" the perfection of the coldness you were trying to measure (E.g. the coldness would be a little warmer than it was before you tried to measure it).

By acknowledging the Observer Effect, we have established that if perfect coldness could exist, we could not know about it (because by "knowing" about it, we make it not perfect anymore). We cannot *experience* perfect coldness. And if there exists something we can never experience, then it may as well not exist at all.

So, we can infer the existence of coldness by talking about heat transfer, but coldness, by itself cannot exist.

It is this overlapping necessary "extantness" and inability to exist that give coldness the quality of being an attribute of Not.

Let's move on to the second precept of Not, darkness.

DARKNESS

There is no such thing as darkness.

"What?" you respond, "Of course there is! It is dark when you turn off the lights. It is dark at night. It is dark inside the refrigerator when the door is closed."

True, it is darker in those places, but just like coldness being a state you can only achieve by the removal of warmth, darkness is a state you can only arrive at by removing light. In any given system, if you remove some light from that system, that system will become darker. As more and more light is removed, the system becomes darker and darker.

If you remove all light from a system, you will be left with pure darkness. The ultimate in darkness. Perfect darkness. Perfection is subjective, but I can still safely say that this darkness I describe would be perfect because there could be nothing darker. There could be no darkness that is darker. In being dark, this darkness – where all light has been removed – is the ultimate achievement in darkness. Thus, it is perfect darkness. And something that is perfect is – well – *perfect.*

Like coldness, you cannot carry darkness around with you and insert it into a system where there is light thereby making that system darker. The only way to make a system darker is by reducing the amount of light in that system. By removing light, you make a room darker. Adding light, makes the room lighter (less dark). We cannot make a room darker by "adding darkness."

It is as if darkness is the canvas on which the room is painted with light. Darkness is the underlying infrastructure "on which" light may exist.

Nowhere in all of existence is there such thing as this perfect darkness I describe. The reason it cannot exist is because there is always, somewhere, a stream or wave of photons (particles of light). Even if it is just a single photon, or a subatomic particle, there is technically energy (a form of light) there.

Imagine, for a moment, you are floating in space somewhere. Can you see stars in the distance? Even stars that might be billions of light years away? If you can see a star – any star – that means there is a stream of photons flooding into your eyes from that star. It means that the space between you and that star has light streaming through it (or at least it did at some point in time). Needless to say, if light is streaming through that space, that space is not "dark."

Nonetheless, let's imagine for a moment that we have created a perfect darkness and now we want to witness it.

If one were to construct a device within which there were no photons, then theoretically one would have created the perfect darkness I describe. But it still could not be detected by the human eye. It could only be known to us through some readout from some device created to detect it. I would posit that where there is molecular activity one will find a photon or quantum influx of energy which can be interpreted as light. Therefore, the detecting of perfect darkness in and of itself would "infect" that darkness with one or more particles of light thereby making it no longer a pure and perfect darkness.

Paradoxically, darkness *must* exist for there to be light, even though darkness without light cannot exist. This is a fundamental aspect of darkness that is difficult to describe. Darkness is to light as a canvas is to a painting. Darkness will always be there, deep beneath the surface of light, waiting to be revealed. In this way, a perfect darkness *must* exist.

Like coldness, darkness is not something we can manipulate directly. Only through light can we understand darkness. And a perfect darkness *cannot* exist. Again, we have a paradox.

Thus, darkness is the second of the four core precepts that make up Not.

STASIS

There is no such thing as stasis.

What is that supposed to mean?

First, what I mean by 'stasis' is a measure of activity. Or, rather, in this case, a measure of inactivity. An active system is not a static system. A system with no activity would be a static system. An absolutely static system would be a system in perfect stasis. Imagine an empty room that has a layer of dust in it. There are no objects in the room and there is no movement in the room. It is completely still. Or is it?

It may appear that way on the surface but this room is not really in stasis. Inside each speck of dust is a cosmic explosion of molecular activity. Within the trillions of molecules in each single dust speck are countless trillions of atoms binding, spinning, attracting and repelling each other. Within the atoms are quintillions more subatomic particles in a quantum dance with each other zinging and whizzing around and these particles have bindings and associations with other particles possibly trillions of light years away in quantum entanglements and other quantum sub-arrangements we have yet to comprehend.

In short, like coldness and darkness, stasis is a concept but not a "thing." In other words, you cannot walk up to an active system and add some "stasis" to make the system less active. You can remove activity from a system to arrive at a static system, but you cannot add stillness, stasis, or "inactivity" to a system to make it less active.

Complete and utter stasis is something that cannot be achieved in actual existence. But, like coldness and darkness, if it could be achieved, a state of absolute stasis would represent a form of absolute perfection.

Why can we not achieve true stasis? A system that is perfectly static would be a system with no molecular activity whatsoever. It would be a system with no atomic activity. A system with no subatomic activity. The reason we cannot achieve this is because ultimately everything is comprised of energy and energy cannot stop being "energetic."

A group of atoms or molecules that have no subatomic activity whatsoever is a theoretical concept at best. It is a state of existence we cannot create or measure. Just like coldness and darkness, an attempt to measure a completely static system would introduce an *active* measuring device, thereby causing activity to enter the system. The theoretical state of 'perfect stasis' would be "infected" with activity and no longer be purely static.

Underlying all activity is "a promise" of stasis, though that promise may never be fulfilled. *Can* never be fulfilled. Stasis is a fundamental base over which activity exists, but activity cannot cease in order to reveal this underlying stasis. Paradoxically, stasis must exist as an underlying stratum to existence itself but cannot exist independently of activity.

Stasis is the third of the four core precepts that make up Not.

This brings us to emptiness.

EMPTINESS

There is no such thing as emptiness. That sounds a little bit mystic, a little bit cosmic and a lot bit metaphysical. But if you have followed along from the previous discussions on the four core precepts that make up Not, you will see immediately how this must be the case.

There cannot be a pure state of emptiness because there must always be something present to discern the emptiness. (If no presence is there to discern the emptiness, how can one know that there was emptiness there to begin with)? And as soon as some presence is there to witness the emptiness, the system is no longer empty.

For this discussion we consider a "presence" to be some conglomeration of atoms. A rock, a tree, a flower, a sun or a person are all things considered to be a "presence." But even smaller groupings of atoms are a presence. Any warmth, light or activity must necessarily also be "a presence." You see, in any given system one considers "empty," if nothing else, there must exist the *presence* of warmth, light or activity. Thus, no system can truly be empty.

Space is not empty. In fact, we already covered the point that space is actually a substance. Going back momentarily to the example we considered in the discussion on darkness, imagine you are floating in space somewhere. Can you see stars in the distance? If you can see a star – any star – (as previously mentioned) then that means, there is a stream of photons flooding into your eyes from that star. This means that the space between you and that star has light streaming through it. It is not empty space.

Like coldness, darkness and stasis, one cannot take emptiness and deliver it to some system of presence(s) to reduce the amount of presence. To arrive at emptiness, you can only remove presence. You cannot add emptiness.

If you could remove all presence from a system you could then achieve a state of absolute and perfect emptiness. The perfection of the emptiness is implicit because a system that contains absolutely no presence would be the ultimate in emptiness. It could not become emptier. If it cannot become emptier, then it is perfectly empty. If nothing else can be removed, it is the pinnacle of emptiness. In this way, the emptiness I describe represents a certain purity. Perfection.

Again, we have the paradox of *required being* (emptiness must exist) overlaid with the inability for the attribute to exist (emptiness cannot exist). It is as if emptiness exists as a fundamental underlying basis for presence to fill. We can imagine emptiness because we know there are places that exist when we are not in those places. But even when we (as presence) are not in those places, there is still warmth, light and activity in those places and for this reason, no place may be truly empty.

Emptiness is the last of the four core precepts that make up Not.

Finally, this discussion of the four core precepts brings us to Not, itself.

NOT

Coldness, darkness, stasis, and emptiness are the four core precepts of Not. As such, Not is simply defined as "cold, dark, static emptiness."

In describing the four core precepts of Not, we have established that none of them are attributes that truly exist. Or, again, if they can exist it doesn't matter to us, because we can never know about their existence.

Thus, the same is true with Not. Not cannot exist. Or, if it can exist, we can never know about it. The experience of Not would change Not into not being Not anymore by the entity which was doing the experiencing.

Not is the canvas on which life is painted using the paints of warmth, light, activity, and presence with the caveat that the paint can never *experience* the canvas.

Underneath all of life, underneath everything that was, is, or can be, there is always this basis of Not, "waiting" to be revealed.

Not is beneath the substrate of reality. Not is the backdrop behind reality. It is the infrastructure on which reality may exist. It is the stratum underlying the cosmos – underlying all of existence.

If you paint a picture of the cosmos and place Not at the bottom, as the basis on which all of reality rests, then there would be nothing depicted underneath Not. Nothing can exist beyond Not. Again, if it did, it would touch Not, thereby changing Not into something that isn't Not.

In this complete lack of anything else, Not is absolute purity and perfection.

◆ ◆ ◆

HOW IS NOT DIFFERENT?

How is the Philosophy of Not different than any of these other religions, philosophies or ideologies that claim absolute knowledge?

It differs in several ways, not least of which is that it provides bricks of belief that may be used to build a deep rooted and unshakeable foundation of belief while at the same time not claiming to provide answers to The Mysteries.

Perhaps even more important, the Philosophy of Not does not pretend absolute knowledge or absolute authority.

Yet, even so, Not does offer us a definitive absolute on which we can build. As we have established, Not is absolute in its "Notness." Nothing can be more "not" that Not. Or said another way, there can be nothing less than Not. It is akin to "absolute zero," but rather it is ***absolute Not***.

You do not have to take my word for it or have faith that I am right. Logic and reason will prevail. Intuition matters too, but it is your logic and reason that I appeal to.

◆ ◆ ◆

PROOF OF LIFE

Now that we have established the existence (or lack of existence) of Not, it may be a good time to address the question of why any of this even matters.

The reason Not matters is not as much rooted in the core precepts of Not as it is in their constituent counterparts: warmth, light, activity, and presence.

If you recall, to arrive at Not, we defined the four core precepts that *do not* exist by removing attributes of our reality that *do* exist.

To achieve coldness, we must remove ***warmth***.
To achieve darkness, we must remove ***light***.
To achieve stasis, we must remove ***activity***.
To achieve emptiness, we must remove ***presence***.

By removing those four attributes in order to define Not, we establish proof of the existence of the very things we removed: warmth, light, activity, and presence. These four attributes had to exist for us to be able to remove them. Thus, warmth, light, activity, and presence are axiomatic. In other words, their existence is proof of their existence. These four attributes can be described as fundamental to all of reality because all of reality is necessarily constructed from them. They are the fundamental building blocks of existence and therefore they are also the fundamental building blocks of Life. Everything that ever was, is, or will be is comprised of warmth, light, activity, and presence.

There are countless ways and reasons one might question reality. For instance, Descartes taught us that we cannot trust our senses and suggested the possibility of a Great Deceiver. But the absolute nature of Not demonstrates to us that if nothing else may be known about our reality, we cannot doubt the existence of warmth, light, activity, and presence.

In order to describe Not, we whittled our way down to the four core precepts of Not by removing the four fundamental building blocks of Life. Now moving in the other direction (using Not as our starting point) we need a word to describe, collectively, the four "lively" counterparts of the four core precepts of Not. I use the word Life (as a proper noun) to collectively describe warmth, light, activity, and presence. Another word that might have worked would be the word, "All," or the word, "Is," as a proper noun. Or any other word that means "everything else." But there was another good reason for me to use the word Life to describe warm, light, active presence. It has to do with the importance of life to all of us who are currently experiencing life.

In considering core values that might be common to all of humanity, life itself must be the most fundamental and universal value we all share. I am talking simply about the importance of living. In fact, life must be *the most* fundamental core value shared between all living beings. And life cannot exist without warm, light, active, presence. Naming this warm, light, active presence, "Life," draws attention to this core life-value which all of us share.

Another thing the word "Life" does is draw attention to just how "not like Life," Not is. In other words, Not is Anti-Life.

In the above discussion on Not, I didn't mention how horrific the idea of Not really is, but it is a concept that can make one feel terror at the though of it. Being trapped in a refrigerator with no light would be a warm picnic compared to Not. The kind of lack of warmth, light, activity, and presence that Not represents is technically worse than death for that which is living. This is because even death is comprised of warm, light, active presence. For most Western thinkers, *not being* is a terrifying prospect. It is difficult for us to imagine not being.

The easiest description is of course to imagine what your life was like before you were born. But even this does not quite convey the feeling because before we were born, the warm, light, active presence that makes up our being was already here. We are just a refactoring of the existing warmth, light, activity, and presence that has existed since the beginning of the universe. Just as, after we die, we will once again be refactored from the warm, light, active presence we were in life to some new configuration of warm, light, active presence. (E.g., Death is merely a transformation of Life.) Not is scary because there is no configuration of warm, light, active presence that can exist within Not.

But the terror of Not is not reserved just for the individual. I am talking about the terror of imagining that *only* Not exists. I am talking about the terror in imagining, all warmth, light, activity, and presence disappearing from the universe. It is for this reason that Not could be described as Anti-Life. And to complete the circle, this idea of Anti-Life kind of suggests the name "Life" to describe what would not be Not.

Thus, in the Philosophy of Not, the word "life," has two different ways of being written and means two different things (though they are very closely related and not far off from what the English language already describes as their meaning).

Life, as a proper noun, is merely everything that isn't Not. First and foremost, of course, this is warm, light, active presence. Beyond those attributes, this includes rocks, stars, the stuff of space, metal, air, dirt, fire, water, flowers, trees and even people.

On top of this base definition, there is another layer of life which is described more along the lines of how an English language dictionary would define it. Life with a lowercase "l" is that which is autonomous, consumes food and reproduces. But I take this definition a step a further and add in the awareness of our own awareness. Religion and spirituality call this the soul or spirit. Science calls it the mind or consciousness. I combine these two ideas into the contraction of spirit-consciousness. As the spirit-consciousness, it is the duality within. The "true self."

◆ ◆ ◆

GOOD & EVIL

Good and evil are human ideas. The sun is not *evil* for burning the face of Mercury any more than the sun is *good* for sustaining life on Earth. The sun just is.

The fact that good and evil are human constructs is important to point out when we are talking about spirit-consciousness and authorization for being coming from within an individual. One of the implications here is that good and evil also can only come from within an individual human being.

Of course, there are billions of other human beings, each one with a spirit-consciousness – each one generating their own wellspring of self-authorization and the good and evil that comes with it.

"Over eight billion individual wellsprings of good and evil, all mixed up across the face of the planet," describes our world surprisingly well.

In brief, I think of evil as behavior we engage in which knowingly harms someone else while (probably) benefitting us, but we do it anyway. This can be as simple and "harmless" as cutting someone off in traffic or not holding the elevator door for someone and can be as egregious as causing personal injury or death to another lifeform (human or otherwise). Goodness, on the other hand is basically that which is not evil.

We are wellsprings of warm, light, active, and present energy. This energy which emanates from us, comes from within us and flows outward whether or not we direct it with intention. Perhaps the source of this energy is our spirit-consciousness, or perhaps the spirit-consciousness is a result of this energy wellspring. Either way, as part of *being* we necessarily authorize ourselves as we perform both good and evil actions in the world around us throughout our daily lives.

Earlier I mentioned the idea of front and back and how this concept is different from the idea of coldness and warmness. As a duality, good and evil are more like front and back. They both must exist, and neither can exist without the other one.

No person can be purely good or purely evil. We are all somewhere within a gray haze when it comes to the Gradient Yin-Yang of good and evil. Thus, we all must navigate a gray path as we move through life trying to do good while avoiding doing evil.

◆ ◆ ◆

THE PRINCIPLES OF NOT

How does one walk the gray path without the scriptures of some religious dogma? How does one establish a moral compass if one does not inherit it from a church or a religion?

How do we choose this job over that one? Should I go with my friends on this road trip or spend the week with my sick aunt? Should I move to the big city? Should I move to the country? Should I have a baby? Should I get married? Should I join the Army? Should I find religion? How do I decide which one to choose?

Should you ask your friends or family for advice, pray to a god or gods, meditate, cast lots, do a tarot reading or flip a coin? Unfortunately, nobody can make the hard choices (or any choices) for you. You must choose. Authorization for action based on your choice comes from within you. Nonetheless, we still need some kind of guide in order to make those important decisions.

The Principles of Not are a guide to decision making. They are "of Not" because Not is the foundation of the philosophy from whence they came.

The principles are almost just plain common sense. They are the things that are most important to all humans and as you read them you will likely be unsurprised by what they are and you may even exclaim, "Well of course, those are the things that matter most."

Putting them in order is what makes them "The Principles of Not" and gives us the ability to use them in decision making. In order of importance, from most important to least, they are:

1. Life
2. Fitness
3. Relationships
4. Personal Code
5. Community

These principles flow in order of precedence – from most important to least important – and as such we can use them to determine what we should do in any given situation.

There are two ways to look at the Principles. On the one hand, these principles can be seen as values and as values (as previously mentioned) you can use them to make decisions. This approach is called Cinereo Modo ("the gray walk"). It is a way one can use the Principles in everyday life. For instance, "should I quit the team?" There are a series of questions you can ask to test the action against the Principles to help you decide what to do.

The other approach to the Principles is called Cinereo Ascensus ("the gray climb"). This is a way of using the Principles to provide direction. Instead of reacting, you are being proactive. Are you in a place where you feel like you have stagnated? Are you feeling spiritually flat? Looking for direction? Cinereo Ascensus uses the Principles in such a way that you can align yourself with the Principles in forward (upward) movement in your life.

Let's quickly touch on each of the five principles:

LIFE (VITA)

There is nothing more important than life. In all of existence; in all the cosmos; in all of imagination and that which was, is and could be, there is nothing more important than life.

Life supersedes all other values.

More important than god(s)? Yes. If you tell your child that some unsubstantiated god (they have no evidence of this god yet) is the most important thing in the world (to them this means "the universe"), then you have planted a seed of an unknown tree. In other words, you may have an idea of what you want that tree to look like, but you cannot control the way that tree is going to grow in their mind. And it is already starting out badly.

Depending on the age of the child and countless other variables, the child is going to start going through life with a child's understanding of "god(s)" and this irreconcilable knowledge that a vague idea of an entity that does not appear to be alive is more important than love, life, relationships, themselves, other people, etc.

As the child grows older and illusions begin to shatter, the solidity of their belief in "what is most important in life" is going to start to falter. Santa Clause is not real?! The Tooth Fairy, too?! The Easter Bunny?! Combine these shocking lies with the whispers from atheists and the secular set that "god(s)" may not be real, and you have a recipe for confusion and self-doubt. By the time the child is old enough to understand what has happened, much damage will have already been done and the child (perhaps now an adult) will have to start from the ground, up, in attempting to ascertain what is most important in life.

An equally poor choice is telling your child that you do not know what is most important in life or telling them that getting good grades and landing a good job is most important in life. These shallow ideals are temporal and can shift out from underneath us at any given moment. If you want to prepare your children for the world, you need to give them a foundation for a structure of believe that cannot be blown away by the first unscrupulous charlatan that comes along seeking to exploit them.

Tell them, "Life is the most important thing in the world." Without even being conscious of it, they will almost instantly see the truth in that statement. As they grow older and other illusions are shattered, they will have this seed of truth you have given them that is solid and real. They will see that "Life is the most important thing in the world," is an unbreakable brick in their foundation of belief upon which they can build a solid structure.

When you hold life as your highest principle, no other ideal can be held higher. What this means is that no group, organization, or entity can convince you to kill somebody merely based on the merit that they think it is a good idea. Most notably this removes the authorization other religions grant to kill in the name of their god or gods. You may not kill because a god told you to. Killing in the name of any religion or deity is unacceptable because life is held as a higher principle than religion and deities. Religion, in fact, is pretty far down the stack when it comes to the hierarchy of principles. (Religion is part of the Community Principle). This also elevates life above the importance of money, material wealth, power over other humans, etc. thus establishing that killing for any reason other than preserving life is unacceptable. When it comes to taking life in order to preserve other life, understandably this can become very complicated.

All life is sacred but human life is the most sacred. The reason for this is twofold. One reason is we must fall well within the laws of mankind and get along with our neighbors and other religions and ideologies and the laws of mankind stipulate that human life has more value than other life. In other words, we must acknowledge human life as more valuable because the laws of the land say so. Another reason is because we generalize that humans are different from the other animals. Humans do things no other animals do including cooking their food, building quantum computers and mega-cities and forming armies to fight and kill each other for ideological reasons instead of simply to protect or provide for ourselves or our young. We are undeniably different from the other animals.

This elevates us, essentially, just because we say so. Humans rule the planet Earth because we say we do. This will remain the status quo until someone or something comes along and knocks us off our throne.

FITNESS (ACIEM EXACUITUR)

In order to enjoy, protect, preserve, and maintain life, we must be fit. Thus, the next most important value is fitness.

Fitness. Working out (physically, mentally, emotionally, spiritually, socially), reading, writing, studying, learning, creating art.

You must keep yourself fit in every way. Keeping fit in every area of life (spiritual, mental, emotional, physical, social) will maximize your ability to enjoy, protect, promulgate, and honor your life and other life. This is where the term "aciem exacuitur" comes in. Aciem exacuitur means "sharpened edge." The second most important Principle of Not is this sharpening of the edge.

From the work of Charles Darwin, came the idea of "survival of the fittest." One of the things we learn from this theory is that only the most fit of any given mutation will survive. Those creatures that are capable of adapting to the changes wrought by nature prove themselves to be more fit and their progeny will survive while those who are less fit perish.

Fitness, in this way, connects back to the first Principle of Not, "life." Only those most fit to survive in life will live. And living is our highest principle. To stay alive. To honor life. By keeping your edge sharp in spirit, mind, and body, you give you and your progeny a better chance of staying alive and adding your own uniqueness to the universe. In this way you honor life.

RELATIONSHIPS (NECESSITUDO)

At the end, when all is said and done, and you look back over your life, that which will have mattered most will be the relationships you have had. Those that you have garnered, those you have squandered, those you have broken up or helped create. Thus, the next most important thing to life and staying fit are your relationships. This discussion on relationships is almost exclusively reserved for relationships between living things.

It is possible that relationships between living and nonliving things is also important. For instance, between a living person and a dearly departed person. But by and large, the relationships between living beings are more important than relationships between non-living beings or anything inanimate.

You should garner and foster relationships wherever possible, but no relationship should ever interfere with the first or second principles. Your own spiritual, mental, emotional, physical, and social fitness is of higher importance than any relationship other than your relationship with Life.

Relationships that interfere with spiritual, mental, emotional, physical, or social fitness should likely be ended. Or at least redefined in order to reduce their negative impact on your life.

PERSONAL CODE (CODICE PERSONALUM)

Your personal code defines your morality. It defines how you act and how you make decisions.

As you move through life, learning more about yourself spiritually, mentally, emotionally, physically, and socially, you learn to love yourself and you develop relationships and become more at peace with yourself in all aspects of life. Over time, as you analyze the varying paradigms that you find on your journey, you will collect these splinters of truth and start to form your personal code. Most everyone has a personal code that guides them though many people do not realize they have constructed one.

One should constantly examine one's personal code. Look for gaps, holes, discrepancies, hypocrisies, etc., and fix them or at the very least make certain you are aware of them as you work toward fixing them. Your personal code will contain some "bricks" of belief but should also have some flux.

Your personal code should help define you as a person. For instance you might say, "I have integrity." Or you may think of yourself as a warrior, a seeker, a student, or a leader. Your code may contain statements about you such as, "I always pay my debts," "I'm an honest person," or even something like, “I want to find myself.”

Over time you should write down some or all of your code. This is something you can hand down to your progeny or pass on to a loved one who could benefit from the inspiration. If you haven't already started working out your personal code, a "personal mission statement" might be a good way to start.

You should identify yourself with your code. Relationships may come and go. Jobs may come and go. Your code cannot be broken or taken away from you. Though your code can change, it can only be changed by you and therefore even in flux, your code is your island in the chaotic storm of everyday life.

You can center yourself around your code. On your code. And therefore, no matter what happens all around you, you will not be lost. You will always know who you are – where you are – what you are. You can always find yourself.

COMMUNITY (CIVITAS)

Community is everything "communal" and also equates to most everything "social." This means being involved in your community. It can be involvement in various organizations such as clubs, associations, religions, fraternities, sororities, societies, etc. This includes what some other systems refer to as "environment," which includes ever widening communal circles such as your town, city, metro area, region, state, country, continent, hemisphere, planet, and solar system. This Principle will reach beyond the solar system when humans can, but for now the outer limits of 'community' are mostly confined to the area between Earth and Mars (and possibly Venus depending on current mission status for the world's space agencies).

The community principle incorporates societal laws, rules, and codes. First, it might be your "house rules," or apartment or condominium rules. Then the local neighborhood covenants, followed by city ordinances, county laws, state laws, federal and then international laws. You should be aware of these rules and laws and try to abide by them. The adherence to such earthly ideals is important in maintaining that thread that has run all the way through from the core, from life through fitness, and through relationships and personal code. These principles are all connected through the self. By adhering to communal rules, laws, and certain dictates, you help maintain your social fitness which reverberates back into physical, emotional, mental, and finally spiritual health. All of these things are interconnected.

This brief overview of the five Principles of Not brings us to the next topic, which is how to engage the Principles in day-to-day living. Thus, we need to discuss The Shallows.

◆ ◆ ◆

THE SHALLOWS

This next part is difficult to address, especially coming away from that last section about the importance of community. On the one hand, Community is of vital importance, but on the other hand, the Community principle melds into the next "level" of society which is the shallow existence of mediocrity and the soul-killing trade of our life-essence for money.

"Soul-killing," may seem a bit dramatic, but many of us have experienced this in our lives and many are experiencing it even now. Personally, I have found a way to trade life for money that works well for my family and me, but it hasn't always been this way. Many times, in my life, I have watched the clock slowly, slowly, slowly tick away one second as I dread how long it will take until the next second finally passes.

This might be a good time to offer the colloquialism, "don't wish your life away." If possible, instead of dreading every passing moment until your shift ends, it would be better to *be* in the moment and feel the world around you. Or imagine ways you can change your situation. Or focus on why you are trading your life for such drudgery and ask yourself if it is still the best way to get what you want. I don't know what to tell you. This miasma of day-in, day-out living is inevitable, and we must each find our own way through it until we can come to a place where we either change it, change ourselves, or find peace with ourselves while still remaining in it.

Don't get me wrong. I love life! And Life! I love being here and when I look back at all the moments of time I "wasted" watching the clock, I do not regret it. It was what it needed to be to get me where I am today, and I am really happy with where I am today and where I am heading. It might be easy to look back and berate myself with something like, "You should not have wasted so many hours 'not being present'," but I completely forgive myself because that is who I was then. That is where I was then.

There is another difficult aspect of The Shallows I need to address. I want to offer this disclaimer before I get into it that I am not a nihilist and I do not regard nihilism as a recommended philosophy of living. Nonetheless, the aspect of The Shallows that I am about to describe sounds extremely nihilistic. It is essentially that none of this matters (gestures at everything all around us).

I am talking about all of these things which make up "society." Rules, laws, streets, cities, religions, schools, etc. None of it matters. None of that stuff matters because it is all illusory. It is all part of the dream of reality that is painted in our minds. Only that which manifests in our minds is truly real. But this knowledge about the illusory nature of everything around us must be taken with a grain of salt, because the following statement is critical to understand:

Money isn't real, but if you don't pay your power bill, they will turn off your electricity.

So, on the one hand, none of this matters, but on the other hand, we have to play the game. As such, it is my recommendation that in The Shallows, you take the reigns (or the ship's wheel, etc.) and direct your course in a way that brings you tranquility, peace, contentment, or whatever else you desire that makes your life feel valid and worthwhile. Direct your life in a way that validates you or *authorizes* you.

You see? It is from The Shallows of the day-to-day drudgery of living life that the need for authorization springs forth. Our plight in daily life is where the question of "Am I okay?" comes from. How could it not? Open up TikTok, or

Facebook, or tap into a newsfeed somewhere and what you will see is complete chaos.

You'll see "over eight billion individual wellsprings of good and evil, all mixed up across the face of the planet," each spewing forth their own understanding of what The Shallows are and the best way to navigate the shallows from their own perspective.

It is from this chaos that one tries to find oneself. It is from this chaos that one seeks authorization for being.

The Principles of Not provide a set of values one can use to make decisions on day-to-day activities – this gives us a "how" to get through the day. But the Principles don't provide a deeper insight into *why* we should keep going. The ideology of Authorism can provide the "why."

◆ ◆ ◆

THE IDEOLOGY OF AUTHORISM

There are two fundamental pillars of Authorism. One is that we author our own lives. This idea can be understood by imagining your life as a written story. Imagine your life as a story with you as the main character. Who is the author of this story? Is it the universe? God(s)? Your parents? Or is it you?

Authorism puts forth the argument that you are the ultimate author of your story. This puts a lot of responsibility on you to come up with a good plot and make up a really good ending, but it also introduces a great deal of liberation in that you are free to write the story as you see fit. If there are scary scenes or disturbing characters in your story, as the author, you can literally write them out. Likewise, if there are intriguing characters or exciting adventures you want in your life, you can write them in.

The second pillar of Authorism is essentially the idea that after food, water, and shelter, what people want most is *authorization* for being. In essence, this means that we do not really feel like we belong here, and we hope to find authorization *for being here* through some external agency. This is usually in the form of gods, religions, or spiritual organizations outside of ourselves. The "outside of ourselves" part is critical to acknowledge because this means that we seek *external authorization* for our being, and this turns out to be folly because we can only find true authorization for being from within ourselves.

No amount of seeking authorization from some external source can complete us because true authorization for being comes from within ourselves. In fact, Authorism goes a step further in saying that those who seem to have found authorization from some external source, have really only used the external source as a trigger to unlock *authorization for being* from within themselves (E.g., self-authorization). Thus, they are actually leaning on this external source and therefore not really getting the true self-authorization they seek.

◆ ◆ ◆

MANIFESTATION

There is one more thing I need to mention before I close this document. Manifestation.

This is one of the many misunderstood ideas in spiritual practice and has been used to describe a great many things (most of the time ambiguously described at best).

There are a handful of things that you cannot really learn about by doing a web search. Manifestation is one of them. It's not because the information isn't out there, it's because there's too much information on the topic out there.

When I talk about 'manifestation,' I am almost always talking about the manifestation of reality through thought.

This is not "creating something from nothing," but rather a guiding of the world around us through thinking. Or perhaps a reconfiguring.

The reason it is possible is because everything that exists outside of us is rebuilt in our minds and it is in our mind where it is all finally *experienced.* This is, in part, how it works. I can explain parts of how it works, but the bottom line is that I do not know *why* it works.

When you alter your experience (in your mind), this reflects back out into the world around you and starts to bend your world into this new paradigm of thought.

I think the reason that there is so much ambiguity out there around 'manifestation' is that anyone who has used it knows it works but none of us really know why it works.

One of the reasons I think we don't know why it works is that we are using the wrong paradigm of thought to behold all of existence, but that is a topic for another paper.

MAGIC, CEREMONY, AND RITUALS

The actual manifestation of thought into reality is taking place at a deeper level. It is the power of manifestation from pure spirit-consciousness directly into reality. I take the liberty of calling this "magic" because neither science nor religion can yet explain it.

When you manifest your own reality directly into the world you do so through self-authorization. If you use a god or magic, Authorism would say this is accomplished through Authorization Loopback.

Let us use healing magic as an example. In the book, *Not Rituals & Ceremonies,* there is a Ritual of Healing. In the Ritual of Healing, the practitioner wishes to manifest healing energy into a person they love who is very far away. This can be done merely by thinking it. However, a visual aid may be helpful. By envisioning a direct line of energy leaving the practitioner and entering the loved one, the healing energy may be more easily broadcast.

The practitioner, however, may not be ready for this kind of power. In that case, the practitioner may wish to invoke a god or use ritual magic. Magic, in short, is a visual aid we use to help us manifest our desires into reality.

The same manifestation of power into the world may be accomplished through the use of thought, gods, magic or religion.

You may wonder what use one could possibly have for magic when each of us knows full well that the power of manifestation comes directly from within. There are several answers but two that I will bring to the forefront. Doing something religiously reinforces that thing in our minds and hearts – in our spirit-consciousness. By practicing "magic" religiously we reinforce those things we hold true and important to us.

Another reason is that just thinking something into existence is sometimes challenging with all of the other distractions of thought which are continuously competing for mind-space. By holding a ritual and invoking certain rites we are able to completely focus on a specific task or end goal with little possibility of distraction. Ritual magic brings us clarity of focus. It is an effective method of sharpening the edge in spirit, mind, emotion and intellect. It teaches us focus and helps sharpen the skill of intention.

Rituals and ceremonies literally improve our overall health much like meditation and prayer have been shown to do in those who practice either or both of those things religiously. During a ritual, one can be completely present and focus on the task at hand thereby letting the worries of the rest of the world slip away.

Daily, weekly, monthly, etc. rituals can become touchstones in our lives, allowing us to reconnect with parts of ourselves that might otherwise drift. Of course it is also enjoyable and gives us something to share with each other but at the same time it provides something deeply personal that we need not share with anyone. You can change yourself and your universe through the power of thought. And it does come from within you. You are the Author of your destiny.

PROOF THAT MANIFESTATION WORKS

Manifestation of reality through thought is absolutely real and is happening all around us and has been happening since before humanity learned to write.

I am going to foreshadow the conclusion of this proof by asking the question, "Is the power of religion real and manifest in this world?"

If you have skimmed over any synopsis of World History, you cannot deny that the power of religion is not only real but has been *the driving force* in shaping human civilization.

Bear with me as we diverge a moment. Do you think the gods, Marduk, Zeus, Ba'al, Odin or Ra are real entities that exist somewhere and have a vested interest in the activities of humans here on Earth?

Most modern readers will respond with something along the lines of, "Of course not. Those are all ancient gods of myth and legend. Everyone knows that those gods are not real!"

Good answer.

What about Jesus, Allah, Krishna, Ahura Mazda or Buddha? Are those real entities that exist somewhere and have a vested interest in the activities of humans here on Earth?

The answer to that question will not come so fast or so definitive. There are people who believe in some of those gods today. Billions of people.

I am not going to try to convince you that any of those gods exist. Nor am I going to try to convince you that any of those gods do not exist. Instead, I am going to draw your attention to that which has been made manifest in our world due to *the power of the belief* in those gods.

The foundation, the structure and the infrastructure of modern human civilization was all built from a religious base. Billions of humans believe in some god or gods.

They believe it so strongly that there are billions of humans who are willing to kill other humans because of the power of their belief. And likewise, there are billions of humans who are willing to die because of the power of their belief.

Any given god of any given religion can be denied, but the power of religion cannot be denied.

Before you argue that it was a god that did it all as opposed to just people believing in a god, I would have to ask you to specify which god it was. Was it Allah? Ahura-Mazda? Jesus? We cannot all agree as to which god it was, can we? But none of us can deny the power of belief.

The power of religion *is* the power of that belief. That which has been made manifest in this world due to the power of religion *is* that which has been made manifest in this world through the power of belief. And belief is thought.

Manifestation of changes in the reality around us are made through thought. The belief in creation causes creation.

◆ ◆ ◆

THE ALCHEMY OF NOT

Wrapping up everything we have just gone through, beginning with who has authority over you, the discussion of organized religion and its claim to absolute knowledge and absolute authority, the Philosophy of Not (and how Not proves the existence of Life), the Principles of Not which then flow from the Philosophy of Not, The Shallows of the day-to-day drudgery of life, then finally the ideology of Authorism and the human concepts of good and evil, we end this document with a method of describing the reality around us. The Alchemy of Not is like an umbrella that covers everything we have already discussed.

The alchemists of old believed they understood a significant part of the universe in that all things were made of air, fire, water, earth, and spirit. They experimented with chemicals and minerals from the earth in attempts to find the underlying connections between all things. They wanted to understand the universe. They wanted to understand *it all.*

The Alchemy of Not is a continuance of that charter. The Alchemy of Not continues this pursuit of a greater understanding of the universe and at the same time offers a praxis which melds day-to-day living with the Philosophy of Not and Authorism.

The Alchemy of Not uses the modern day Not Philosophies but also dips into the occult in order to enrich our practice and provide a method of including ritual and ceremony into our daily living.

◆ ◆ ◆

CONCLUSION

There are many more tangents I would like to explore and many aspects of Authorism and the Philosophy of Not I have had to leave unexplained for now, just as there is much more to say about the Principles and Alchemy of Not. But, alas, there will be another time for those discussions. For this paper, I wanted to focus on Not and Authorism and I feel I have given a fair introductory overview of both.

I would like to thank you, the reader, for your time, and encourage you to never stop seeking answers.

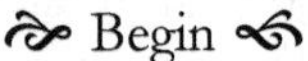

www.ingramcontent.com/pod-product-compliance
Lightning Source LLC
LaVergne TN
LVHW010544100826
845148LV00013B/2596

* 9 7 8 1 7 3 7 2 7 5 0 1 5 *